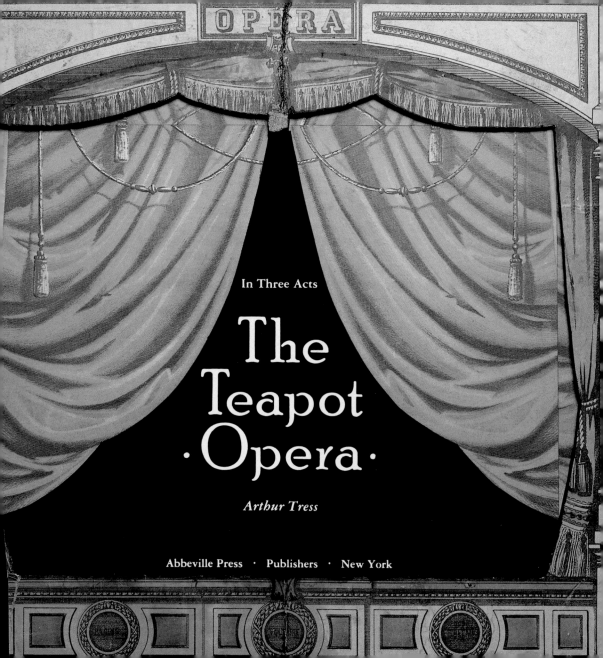

In Three Acts

The Teapot ·Opera·

Arthur Tress

Abbeville Press · Publishers · New York

· *To Mother* ·

Editor: Alan Axelrod
Designer: Renée Khatami
Production manager: Dana Cole

Copyright 1988 by Arthur Tress

Published in the United States of America in 1988 by
Abbeville Press, Inc.

Printed and bound in Singapore
First edition

Original signed color prints are available from
Arthur Tress, 2 Riverside Drive,
New York, NY 10023

Jewelry by Billy Boy™

Library of Congress Cataloging-in-Publication Data
Tress, Arthur.
Teapot opera in three acts.
Contents: Act 1, The birth of ideas—Act 2,
The voyage—Act 3, The final judgment.
1. Photography, Artistic.   I. Title.
TR654.T726   1988   779'092'4   87-35073
ISBN 0-89659-815-2

Act 3 completed with the assistance of
the MacDowell Colony.

Program

ACT I
· The Birth of Ideas ·

Before the invention of Magic,
there was only the dark Sea.

Then, all of a sudden,
a Teapot appeared,

out of which sprang
a great Stallion,

whose first leap sparked
the celestial Spheres,

the Planets,

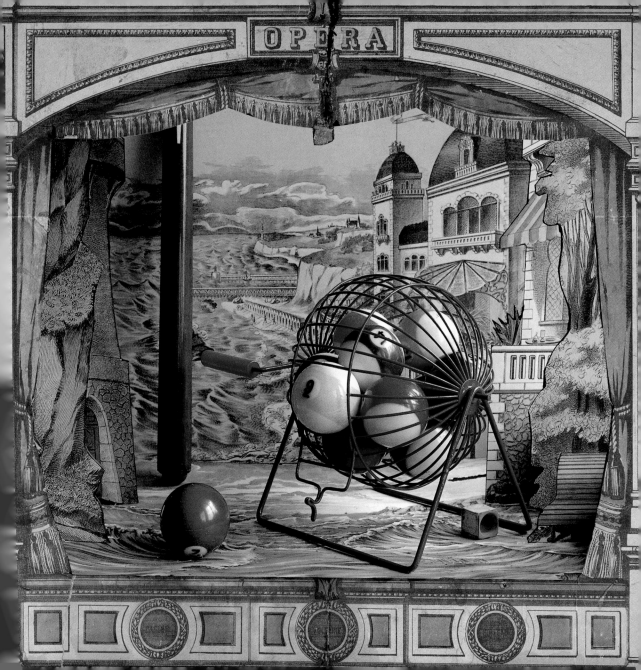

*the Sun, the Moon,
and the Seasons,*

which in turn gave birth
to Strife,

Beauty,

Death,

and myriad Ideas
that touched the Mind,

multiplied, and overflowed
upon the Ocean.

ACT II
· The Voyage ·

The Ideas embarked upon
a Journey

and one day set foot upon
an exotic Island,

where they came upon
fantastic Creatures

34

*and strange
botanical Species.*

They stumbled upon dark Altars
hinting of strange Rites,

and mysterious Ceremonies
performed by masked Maidens.

Ascending a steep path,
they slipped by the Mountain King

and followed a thread
of Ice

past an ancient
desert Tower

to explore a City buried
in the sand,

where they discovered
antique Manuscripts

(to be read by
kerosene Lamp)

that told of Heroes
who had come before,

of marble Palaces and
historic Deeds,

of the achievements of
great Civilizations,

*and Ideas that died
for a Cause.*

*At last they entered
the underground Chamber,*

where the Magician transformed
them into a great Jewel.

The Final Judgment

*The Court weighed
the magician's Work*

and found him guilty
of Speculation.

Ushered away under
Special Guard,

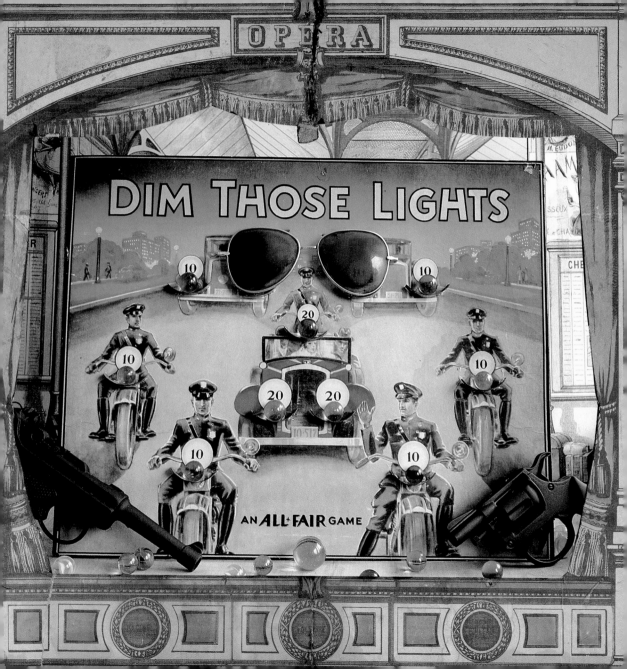

he found himself imprisoned
by his own Illusions

and had a Vision of
sweeter years.

*Brooding, he recalled
the Oracle's words . . .*

"Our darkest Griefs may hold
our brightest Hopes."

But Life still seemed
cold and dim;

so he departed on
another Track

and returned to the Source
of Dreams

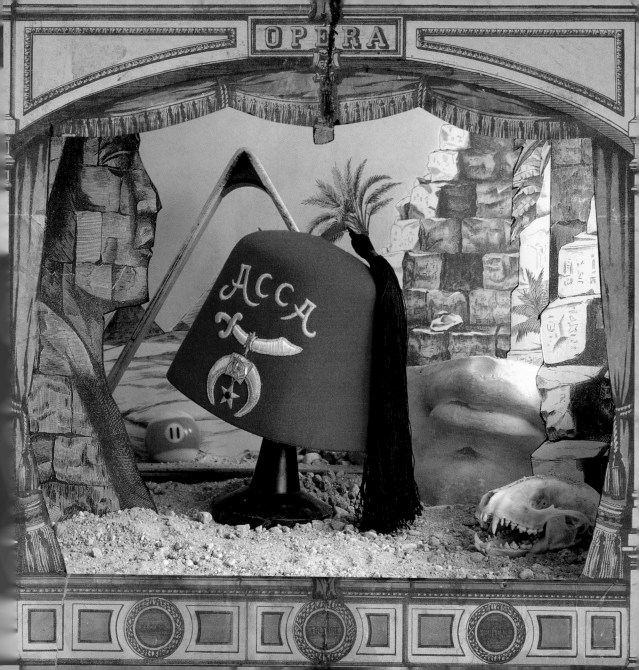

to await the return
of Spring.

A distant Voice
finally broke the Spell,

and he began again to piece together
the intricate pattern of the Stars.

· Afterword ·

The Teapot Opera started in 1965, when I was living in Stockholm. There I had my first job, producing filmstrips for Swedish schoolchildren on the cultural and religious life of various primitive peoples. I traveled, and I documented several groups, including the Lapps, Dogon, and Todas, recording their rituals, dances, and folklore.

One gray winter day I was wandering through the narrow medieval streets of Stockholm's old town when I stumbled upon a curiosity shop run by an elderly Englishman who had somehow settled in Scandinavia. He sold all kinds of dusty bric-a-brac to the occasional tourist. A compulsive pack rat, I thought the tomblike store was an amazing archaeological find—full of dark corners with hidden treasures waiting to be brought to light. Coming through the door, I was filled with anxious anticipation. One of my most frequently recurring dreams is being caught in the act of plundering just such an ancient vault, my arms filled with picture books and dolls. I am never apprehended by the rightful owners, but I must compete for the treasure against other looters. Actually, the proprietor of this shop was quite friendly and let me poke about freely in the dark corners. On one cracked wall he had tacked several unusual paper cut-out puppets articulated at the joints with fasteners. These comical, tricksterlike figures had such strange manic expressions that one could easily imagine them coming to life again after the shop had closed for the night. The owner explained that the figures were originally hung from Christmas trees and later became toys that were suspended near children's beds. When the string attached to them was pulled, their arms and legs spun madly. The figures were originally printed on large sheets bought for a few pennies and were then pasted down on cardboard, cut out, and assembled. They

reminded me of Chinese or Mayan paper fetish figures used in rites of healing and for household protection. Since I was always on the lookout for remnants of ancient ritual in contemporary life, I was delighted to find such tangible demonstrations of pagan emotion, a fascinating combination of the demonic and the beneficial.

I ended up buying a few of these figures every week or so until I had accumulated a collection of about sixty. I called them "the puppet people." The shopkeeper, sensing my love of the bizarre, pulled out a mildewed portfolio containing several large sheets covered with brightly colored drawings. They turned out to be the backdrops for a set of toy theaters. Starting around the 1830s, small paper theaters were printed up as pastimes for Victorian children. They often came with books of plays, stage directions, and casts of characters. The first complete outfit I eventually purchased was produced by "Imagerie Pelligren" in Paris about 1870 and consisted of two dozen combinations of various sets—La Chateau, Le Cirque, Le Bateau, La Mer, and so on. Such toys were also produced in Germany, England, and Italy; over time, I gathered more than a hundred. Of particular interest were those done in Nuremburg, with beautiful chromolithography executed in extraordinarily realistic detail. They reflected the prevailing taste for highly romantic Wagnerian opera-set design.

On some dark Swedish nights, I set up my toy opera on the kitchen table and invited several friends for a theatrical entertainment. I placed two small candles behind the cardboard proscenium; like nineteenth-century footlights, they produced a flickering illumination. While I played some sentimental orchestral piece on my phonograph, my guests and I acted out improvised dramas, holding between our fingers the small cardboard figures, who danced about the stage in surrealistic ballets.

It wasn't until almost twenty years later in my Riverside Drive studio that I once again set up my toy opera. For the preceding few months I had been working on a still-life series for a book of photographs to be called *Nature Morte*. Many of them were done outdoors in various western landscapes: Utah, Arizona, and California. I would go to yard sales and thrift shops, filling up the trunk of my rented car with suburban cast-offs, which I later arranged in elaborate compositions against the background of the snowy mountains and dusty deserts of our national parks. I wanted to show an intersection of manmade objects with the natural world and suggest the interchangeability of the fabricated and the organic. Previously, I had photographed people exclusively; the idea of making inanimate things come alive was a new challenge.

One winter day in New York, when the weather prevented my working outside, I was poking around my studio, trying to find something to occupy myself indoors, when I remembered the old opera stage long stored away in its gray manila envelope. I excitedly reconstructed it on a table near my window. At first I simply placed a few random objects on the empty stage, a 1920s oil can, a giant coin bank in the shape of a Roosevelt dime, and a nineteenth-century Spanish key. In the bluish light of the window, against the cardboard background of a French seaside resort, they were instantaneously animated, each with its own personality, each a character in a play.

That quiet December afternoon was the beginning: I would spend the next few years and hundreds of rolls of film on this project.

In 1973 I had published a book called *Shadow*, a novel in photographs. It was an extended sequence of some ninety-five images of my own shadow shot around the world. The book was meant to be the narrative of my search for identity and style as a photographer, a narrative overlaid with the structure of a visionary voyage of initiation based upon ethnographical studies of shamanistic out-of-the-body experiences. Over the years I had wanted to do another such narrative but had not chanced upon a stimulating motif. Then with the toy playhouse right before me, it suddenly became clear that *this* is what I had been looking for. I would do an opera, a three-act opera with the miscellaneous household and antique objects I had collected over the years serving as singers.

But what would the libretto be? I struggled with several outlines, and then I saw it, too, right before me. The story would be what had just happened: the sudden coming together of accidental elements, the surprising burst of energy, the flash of insight that sparks a work of the imagination.

There was still the need to put this raw notion into a more definite shape. Almost every culture has its creation myths. My libretto became an account of how an artist creates, a process parallel to a host of archaic creation myths. The opening of the opera—onto a stage occupied by billowing waves but otherwise empty—is similar to a Tibetan creation myth; the appearance of the teapot that splits apart to reveal a shining white stallion has parallels with the Hindu "cosmic egg"; the transmutation of the stallion into the planets, sun, moon, and other elements of creation recalls the account of genesis found in Hesiod's *Theogony*.

From this interaction between autobiographical narrative and archetypical patterns, I have attempted to address many kinds of situations and human needs—not just my own—in a universal allegory. That is my *Teapot Opera*.